EXPLORING
AMERICA'S REGIONS

EXPLORING THE
MID-ATLANTIC

BY SAMANTHA S. BELL

CONTENT CONSULTANT
Richard Bell, PhD
Associate Professor of History
University of Maryland, College Park

Cover image: The United States Capitol Building is
located in Washington, DC.

Core Library

An Imprint of Abdo Publishing
abdopublishing.com

abdopublishing.com

Published by Abdo Publishing, a division of ABDO, PO Box 398166, Minneapolis, Minnesota 55439. Copyright © 2018 by Abdo Consulting Group, Inc. International copyrights reserved in all countries. No part of this book may be reproduced in any form without written permission from the publisher. Core Library™ is a trademark and logo of Abdo Publishing.

Printed in the United States of America, North Mankato, Minnesota
092017
012018

THIS BOOK CONTAINS
RECYCLED MATERIALS

Cover Photo: Orhan Cam/Shutterstock Images
Interior Photos: Orhan Cam/Shutterstock Images, 1; Hutch Photography/Shutterstock Images, 4–5, 33; Shutterstock Images, 9, 18–19, 23, 43, 45; Red Line Editorial, 10; North Wind Picture Archives, 12–13; Crossroads Creative/iStockphoto, 21; Tom Reichner/Shutterstock Images, 24–25; ER Degginger/Science Source, 28; Edwin Remsberg/VWPics/AP Images, 30–31; George Sheldon/ Alamy, 36–37

Editor: Maddie Spalding
Imprint Designer: Maggie Villaume
Series Design Direction: Ryan Gale

Publisher's Cataloging-in-Publication Data

Names: Bell, Samantha S., author.
Title: Exploring the Mid-Atlantic / by Samantha S. Bell.
Description: Minneapolis, Minnesota : Abdo Publishing, 2018. | Series: Exploring America's regions | Includes online resources and index.
Identifiers: LCCN 2017946941 | ISBN 9781532113819 (lib.bdg.) | ISBN 9781532152696 (ebook)
Subjects: LCSH: Atlantic Coast (Middle Atlantic States)--Juvenile literature. | Discovery and exploration --Juvenile literature. | Travel--Juvenile literature. | United States--Historical geography--Juvenile literature.
Classification: DDC 917.40--dc23
LC record available at https://lccn.loc.gov/2017946941

CONTENTS

SMALL AND SIMPLE, BIG AND BUSY

A family in a horse-drawn buggy rides slowly along a country road in Lancaster County, Pennsylvania. They are part of a religious community known as the Amish. Their buggy passes farmhouses, barns, and a one-room schoolhouse. Just 150 miles (240 km) away, crowds of people make their way through the streets of New York City. Cars, taxis, and buses inch forward through traffic jams. Skyscrapers tower over the city. Billboards light up the streets.

There are many Amish farming communities in Lancaster County, Pennsylvania.

PERSPECTIVES
THE SIMPLE LIFE

Pennsylvania has the second-largest Amish population in the United States after the state of Ohio. The Amish are a religious farming community. They live much like their ancestors did hundreds of years ago. They wear plain clothes. They do not use tractors in their fields. Many do not drive cars or use electricity. They do not own televisions, radios, or computers. They believe these modern things would distract them from their faith. The Amish think outside influences could also harm their simple way of life. By living apart from the rest of society, they can keep their communities close.

The two places could not be more different. But both are favorite tourist spots in the Mid-Atlantic. This region follows the Atlantic Coast from New York State to Washington, DC. It also includes the states of Pennsylvania, New Jersey, Delaware, and Maryland.

CLIMATE

Summer days in the Mid-Atlantic region are hot and humid. Temperatures usually hover around

85 degrees Fahrenheit (30°C). Temperatures are even warmer near the coast, as Atlantic Ocean currents carry warm water up from the equator. Further inland, mountain ranges such as the Appalachians block coastal air. This keeps temperatures more moderate.

The Great Lakes also affect temperatures in northern New York and Pennsylvania. The lake water absorbs heat in the summer and releases it during the cooler months. This causes cooler springs and warmer autumns. It can also cause lake effect snow. This occurs

NOR'EASTERS

Nor'easters are strong storms that often hit the Mid-Atlantic. They form in the Gulf of Mexico when warm air from the ocean clashes with cold air from the north. The storms then move up the Atlantic Coast. Northeasterly winds blow in from the ocean ahead of the storms, giving the storms their name. Though nor'easters can hit at any time during the year, they are most violent between September and April. They bring large amounts of rain, ice, or snow. Sometimes they bring a combination of all three.

when cold, dry air picks up moisture and heat by passing over a warm lake.

Residents in the Mid-Atlantic see a lot of other precipitation throughout the year. Almost half of Delaware's days are rainy. Regular snowfalls are common throughout the region in winter.

POPULATION

Delaware is the smallest state in the region. It is only 2,044 square miles (3,289 sq km) in area. It has a population of approximately 950,000 people. Pennsylvania and New York have the largest populations of all the states in the Mid-Atlantic. They also have two of the largest cities in the United States. Pennsylvania has more than 12 million residents. The city of Philadelphia in Pennsylvania has more than 1.5 million residents. This makes it the sixth-largest city in the United States. Nearly 20 million people live in

New York City is the largest city in the United States.

THE MID-ATLANTIC
REGION

This map shows the states in the Mid-Atlantic region. Based on this map, what do you think are the major industries in the region?

N
W · E
S

NEW YORK

●Syracuse ●Albany

●Buffalo

PENNSYLVANIA

Harrisburg Trenton

●New York City

●Pittsburgh

Baltimore

Philadelphia

NEW JERSEY

●Atlantic City

Dover

WASHINGTON, DC

DELAWARE

Annapolis

MARYLAND

ATLANTIC OCEAN

New York State. New York City has more than 8 million residents. This makes it the largest city in the country.

Washington, DC, is not a state. It is a 68-square mile (176-sq km) federal district. The Washington, DC, federal district is an area set aside for the United States government. Washington, DC, was established as the nation's capital in 1790. There are many important government buildings in the area. These include the Capitol where Congress meets and the White House where the president works and lives. Approximately 700,000 people live in Washington, DC.

The Mid-Atlantic is a region of mountains, lakes, and coastline. Some people live in large cities, whereas others live in small towns or quiet neighborhoods. People can enjoy country living on a farm or the salty air at the beach. The Mid-Atlantic has something to offer everyone.

SETTLEMENT AND HISTORY

The first people in the Mid-Atlantic region were Native Americans. There were two main language groups when the Europeans arrived. The Algonquian language group included the Lenni-Lenape tribes in present-day New Jersey, New York, Delaware, and Pennsylvania. It also included the Mahican and Shawnee tribes in present-day Pennsylvania and the Nanticoke and Piscataway tribes in the present-day Chesapeake Bay region. The Iroquoian language group included many tribes. Most lived in present-day New York and

In the 1600s, many Native Americans lived in dwellings called longhouses.

northern Pennsylvania. These included the Cayuga, Mohawk, Oneida, and Seneca tribes. Many Native Americans lived in small, independent communities.

In the early 1600s, European colonists began arriving in the Mid-Atlantic region. The colonists came from the Netherlands, Sweden, and Great Britain. Many Europeans settled on Native American lands. This often led to conflicts. Settlers also brought new diseases. Many Native Americans died. European settlers forced others out of their homelands and onto reservations.

THE FRENCH AND INDIAN WAR

In the mid-1700s, France and England both had colonies in the New World. Tensions increased as each country tried to gain more land. War broke out in 1754. The French colonists, the Lenni-Lenape, and other tribes fought against the English colonists and the Iroquois. When the war ended in 1763, Britain gained all of the French territory east of the Mississippi River.

A NEW COUNTRY

The Mid-Atlantic region played

an important role in the early years of the United States. Independence Hall is located in Philadelphia, Pennsylvania. The Declaration of Independence was signed in 1776 in Independence Hall. In 1789, the Constitution was also signed in Independence Hall. It laid out the rules for the federal government and defined the rights of US citizens.

Up until the mid-1800s, most black people in the United States were enslaved. In the Mid-Atlantic region, some worked in the fields and homes of slaveholders.

PERSPECTIVES
SOLOMON NORTHUP

Solomon Northup was born a free black man in 1808 in New York. In 1841, he traveled to Washington, DC. He was kidnapped and sold to a slaveholder in Louisiana. He was enslaved in the South for 12 years. After he escaped, he wrote a book about his experiences. He wrote: "So we passed, hand-cuffed and in silence . . . through the Capital of a nation, whose theory of government, we are told, rests on the foundation of man's inalienable right to life, LIBERTY, and the pursuit of happiness!"

In Mid-Atlantic cities, enslaved people often worked in shipyards and warehouses. But some people in the northern states wanted enslaved people to be freed. Disagreements between the northern and the southern states about slavery led to the Civil War (1861–1865).

CHANGES

Following the Civil War, the practice of slavery was made illegal. The Mid-Atlantic experienced another major change. Industrialization took off at a fast rate. Many farmers moved to cities. They found better-paying jobs in urban areas and manufacturing centers. Railroads made it easier to transport goods and people. Steel and oil companies became a major source of employment.

In 1892, the federal government opened an immigration station on New York's Ellis Island. Millions of immigrants stopped there before entering the United States. They could see the Statue of Liberty nearby. The statue represented freedom and opportunities they never had before.

STRAIGHT TO THE
SOURCE

When Mary Gordon was 19 years old, she left her family in Ireland to come to the United States. She arrived in New York in 1925 and wrote about her experience:

> Then when we landed in New York, oh, everybody was on deck. So it was kind of nice by the time the ship got into New York. At first, I thought [it] was so hot, I just thought I'd never stand it.
>
> Of course, the clothes that I had were suited for Ireland, because Ireland's climate is different. . . . [New York looked] like fairyland. You could see the cars on the thruways. . . . And the Statue of Liberty. I heard about the Statue of Liberty when we were in school. To actually see it, I couldn't wait to write home.

> Source: Dr. Janet Levine. "Mary Margaret Mullins Gordon." *National Parks Service*. National Parks Service, April 24, 1998. Web. Accessed May 3, 2017.

Consider Your Audience

Read the text carefully. Think about how you would adapt it for a younger friend or sibling. Write a blog post expressing the same information to your new audience. How does your post differ from the original text? Why?

FAMOUS LANDMARKS

People from all around the world recognize the Statue of Liberty. It is a famous landmark in the Mid-Atlantic. But the region has other influential landmarks as well.

MAN-MADE LANDMARKS

The Brooklyn Bridge is a famous suspension bridge in New York. It connects Manhattan with Brooklyn. People can drive, bike, or walk across the bridge. Approximately 150,000 vehicles and pedestrians cross this bridge every day

The Brooklyn Bridge is one of New York City's most well-known landmarks.

PERSPECTIVES

REBUILDING THE BOARDWALK

Boardwalks are walkways that overlook the ocean. They can be found in Mid-Atlantic cities along the coast. In 2012, Hurricane Sandy destroyed parts of many of them, including the Rockaway Boardwalk in New York. Approximately five miles (8 km) of the boardwalk were damaged. Residents told city planners how important the boardwalk was to them. Many people moved to the area because of the beach and the boardwalk. In 2017, the new boardwalk was finally completed. This time, it is made out of concrete instead of wood. It includes colored ramps and a bike lane. The residents helped decide much of the new design.

Washington, DC, has many famous landmarks. Some are located on the National Mall. The Washington Monument is a marble obelisk. It was built to honor George Washington. The Lincoln Memorial is also on the mall. It contains a marble statue of former president Abraham Lincoln.

NATURAL LANDMARKS

The Mid-Atlantic also has many natural landmarks. Niagara Falls is made up of

THE NATIONAL
MALL

This diagram of the National Mall shows the locations of many of the memorials and monuments in Washington, DC. What events and people do these memorials and monuments honor? Why do you think it is important that they were built in the country's capital city?

THE APPALACHIAN TRAIL

The Appalachian Trail is the longest hiking trail in the world. It is 2,190 miles (3,524 km) long. The trail goes from Georgia to Maine. It crosses through all of the Mid-Atlantic states except Delaware. The Appalachian Trail was first proposed in 1921. It was finally completed in 1937. It crosses bogs and wetlands. Some parts are easy to walk along, whereas others are steep climbs.

three waterfalls on the border between New York and Canada. They are American Falls, Bridal Falls, and Horseshoe Falls. Millions of people visit Niagara Falls each year.

The Mid-Atlantic region is mountainous. One important mountain range is the Catskill Mountains. This range is in New York. The Catskill Mountains are a part of the Appalachian Mountain range. Within the Catskills are two large reservoirs. They provide most of the freshwater for New York City.

Another popular place to visit is Chesapeake Bay. Chesapeake Bay lies off the coast of Maryland and

People from all over the world visit Niagara Falls each year.

Virginia. It is the largest estuary in the United States. Baltimore, Maryland, is one of the most important ports on the bay.

Pine Creek Gorge is another natural landmark. It is often called "the Grand Canyon of Pennsylvania." It is almost 50 miles (80 km) long and more than 1,000 feet (305 m) deep.

Landmarks in the Mid-Atlantic draw millions of tourists to the region each year. These man-made structures and natural features make this region unique.

PLANTS AND ANIMALS

The Mid-Atlantic landscape includes mountains, wetlands, and coastal areas. These places are home to a variety of plants and animals.

PLANTS

The Mid-Atlantic has more than 3,000 species of flowering plants. One of these is the eastern redbud tree. This tree can be found in forested areas across the Mid-Atlantic, from southern Pennsylvania to Maryland. In early spring, pink or purple flowers bloom on bare branches. In April and May, heart-shaped leaves appear.

A chipping sparrow rests on an eastern redbud tree in Pennsylvania.

THE NATIONAL CHERRY BLOSSOM FESTIVAL

Each spring, the National Cherry Blossom Festival is held in Washington, DC. Visitors come to see the cherry trees that bloom in the nation's capital. Approximately 3,750 cherry trees can be found in Washington, DC's parks. These trees are not native to the area. They were given as a gift from Japan in 1912. Today, thousands of people visit Washington, DC, each year to see their pink flowers.

American beech trees grow in all of the Mid-Atlantic states. They can be found in forests and open areas. They have large trunks with light grey bark. Beech trees can live for 300 to 400 years and grow up to 80 feet (24 m) tall.

Another common tree in the Mid-Atlantic is the eastern hemlock. The eastern hemlock is the state tree of Pennsylvania. It is an evergreen tree that grows mainly in shaded areas throughout the Mid-Atlantic. These trees can grow to be more than 100 feet (31 m) tall and can live for more than 800 years.

ANIMALS

Many notable animals in the Mid-Atlantic region can be found in the waters along the coast. Blue crabs live in Chesapeake Bay throughout the year. Part of a blue crab's body is bright blue. A blue crab has three pairs of walking legs and one set of paddle-shaped legs. These paddle-shaped legs make it an excellent swimmer. For fishers, these crabs are the most valuable catch in the bay.

Blue crabs can be found along the coast in the Mid-Atlantic.

Eastern hognose snakes can be found in every
Mid-Atlantic state. These snakes have upturned snouts.
They use their snouts to dig up prey such as toads in
the dirt. When threatened, they puff out the skin around

their necks. If this does not scare away their attacker, they will roll over and play dead.

The wildlife of the Mid-Atlantic is as varied as the region's landscapes. It is all part of the natural beauty of the region.

EXPLORE ONLINE

Chapter Four talks about the blue crabs in Chesapeake Bay. The article at the website below gives more information about these crabs. As you know, every source is different. How is the information from the website the same as the information in Chapter Four? What new information did you learn from the website?

ABOUT THE BLUE CRAB

abdocorelibrary.com/exploring-mid-atlantic

MAKING MONEY

Residents of the Mid-Atlantic region earn livings in many different ways. Some rely on natural resources. Others are part of growing industries.

FROM THE LAND AND SEA

In some parts of the Mid-Atlantic, mining has been a major source of income. Some mines are dug for coal. Approximately 400 people are employed in the coal mining industry in Maryland. Northern Pennsylvania has the country's largest supply of anthracite, a hard coal used for heating. Mines in New Jersey and New York produce stone, sand, and gravel.

Workers haul oysters onboard a fishing vessel in Chesapeake Bay.

FARMING FOR GENERATIONS

Since 1867, six generations of the Bennett family have worked on the same farm in Frankford, Delaware. In the past, they raised grain, turkeys, and chickens. In 1982, they planted their first peach trees. Today, the family sells peaches and blueberries. Hail Bennett is the present owner. He went to college in South Carolina. But his love for farming drew him back to Delaware. He now works on the Bennett family farm and keeps his family's farming legacy alive.

These materials are used for building houses and other types of construction. Sand is also used for making glass.

The farming industry in the Mid-Atlantic has declined through the years. The growth of cities and high land prices have led to the loss of some farmlands. But farming remains an important industry.

Many farms in the region are owned by families. Farmers grow a variety of fruits and vegetables. They also raise chickens, hogs, and cows. Dairy farms provide

Amish farmers gather corn in rural Pennsylvania.

income to many farmers in Pennsylvania, New York, and Maryland.

For many years, commercial fishing has been part of the economy of Maryland, especially the Chesapeake Bay region. Some fishing communities host seafood and

NEW YORK CITY'S FINANCIAL DISTRICT

New York City's Financial District is located in lower Manhattan. It includes Wall Street, where the New York Stock Exchange is located. Investors at the New York Stock Exchange buy and sell millions of stocks every day. The Financial District is also the headquarters of large investment banks. But it is a community, too. It is a center for music, dance, and art events. The National 9/11 Memorial and 9/11 Tribute Center are also in the Financial District. They honor the lives lost to the terrorist attacks on New York City's World Trade Center on September 11, 2001.

fishing festivals. Others provide visitors with recreational saltwater fishing trips.

BIG BUSINESS

Tourism is another important industry in the Mid-Atlantic. The region attracts tourists from all over the world. Tourism creates jobs in hotels, restaurants, stores, and museums. Washington, DC, attracts approximately 20 million tourists each year. In 2016, New York City welcomed more than 60 million visitors.

The Chesapeake Bay area offers recreational activities for tourists. Popular activities include boating, camping, and swimming. Visitors to Pennsylvania can explore the state's many history museums.

Another growing industry in the Mid-Atlantic is financial services. New York City's Financial District has been the center of the country's financial industry for many years. In Delaware and New Jersey, the financial industry has also created thousands of jobs.

FURTHER EVIDENCE

Chapter Five discusses the economy of the Mid-Atlantic region. Identify one of the chapter's main points. What evidence does the author provide to support this point? Read the article about industries in New York State at the website below. Does the information on the website support this point? Or does it present new evidence?

NEW YORK STATE INDUSTRIES

abdocorelibrary.com/exploring-mid-atlantic

LIFE IN THE MID-ATLANTIC

People from many different places have made the Mid-Atlantic region their home. Today, the region is a mix of cultures unlike any other.

NATIVE AMERICAN COMMUNITIES

Many of the Native American tribes that once lived in the Mid-Atlantic now live on reservations in other parts of the country. But a small group of the Lenni-Lenape tribes still lives in the region. Eight federally recognized Native American tribes live in New York State. Many of them live in cities. Others live on or

Native Americans teach about their cultures at a replica 1600s village in Lancaster County, Pennsylvania.

near reservations. In Maryland, the Accohannock tribe is one of the oldest tribes. The Accohannock people created a traditional Native American village to preserve the tribe's history, language, and culture. The village teaches visitors about the Accohannock tribe.

REGIONAL FLAVORS

Many other people in the Mid-Atlantic also work to preserve their heritages. One way that they do so is through the food they make. Immigrants from Italy brought recipes for pasta, pizza, and seafood dishes. New York has more Italian Americans than any other US state. Many traditional Italian restaurants can be found in the neighborhood of Little Italy in Manhattan, New York.

Jewish immigrants from Europe have also influenced Mid-Atlantic flavors. New York has more Jewish people than any other US state. Many traditional Jewish dishes have become popular in the Mid-Atlantic region, including bagels and lox. Lox is salmon that is smoked or preserved in salt.

New York City has the largest Chinese population of any US city. In the mid- to late 1800s, thousands of Chinese immigrants settled in New York. They formed a community in New York City that became known as Chinatown. Today, the area is home to traditional Chinese restaurants and food markets. Philadelphia's Chinatown is also a thriving, historic neighborhood.

THE SMITHSONIAN

The Smithsonian Institution is the world's largest museum complex and research center. It includes 19 museums and galleries as well as a zoo and gardens. The National Museum of the American Indian George Gustav Heye Center and the Cooper Hewitt, Smithsonian Design Museum are in New York City. Most other Smithsonian complexes are in or near Washington, DC. Smithsonian museums display nearly 140 million objects from around the world.

THE ARTS

The Mid-Atlantic is also famous for its arts culture. New York City is home to many well-known arts institutions. One is the Julliard School. Students come from all over the world to study music, dance, and drama there. Another is the New York City Ballet.

With all there is to see and do in the Mid-Atlantic, it is no wonder so many people want to visit the region. It is also easy to understand why many people want to live there. Both tourists and residents have so much to explore and experience.

STRAIGHT TO THE
SOURCE

Holland Cotter is an art critic who writes for the *New York Times*. He explains how the Metropolitan Museum of Art in New York City can reach a new generation of visitors:

> *What I can talk about is art, and how a museum can make people care about it. If historical art is now a hard sell, and it is, learn to sell it hard. That means, among other things, start telling the truth about it: about who made objects, and how they work in the world, and how they got to the museum, and what they mean, what values they advertise, good and bad. Go for truth (which, like the telling of history, is always changing), and connect art to life. Mix things up: periods, functions, cultures. (You can always unmix them.) Let audiences see that old is always new, if viewed through knowledge.*

> Source: Holland Cotter. "How to Fix the Met: Connect Art to Life." *New York Times*. New York Times, March 1, 2017. Web. Accessed May 3, 2017.

Point of View
Cotter believes that historic art can be meaningful to young people. What does he say will get them interested in art? Do you agree? Why or why not?

FAST FACTS

- Total Area: 124,295 square miles (200,033 sq km)

- Population: Approximately 49 million people

- Largest City: New York City, New York

- Largest State by Population: New York

- Smallest State by Population: Delaware

- Largest State by Land Size: New York

- Smallest State by Land Size: Delaware

- Highest Point: Mount Marcy in New York, 5,344 feet (1,629 m) above sea level

- Lowest Points: Chesapeake Bay in Maryland and the Delaware River in Pennsylvania, at sea level, 0 feet (0 m)

- History: Delaware was named after Virginia's governor, Lord De La Warr.

- Animals: Delaware Bay is home to more horseshoe crabs than anywhere else in the world.

- Landmarks: Adirondack Park in New York is larger than Yellowstone, Everglades, Glacier, and Grand Canyon national parks combined.

STOP AND
THINK

Dig Deeper

After reading this book, what questions do you still have about the Mid-Atlantic region? With an adult's help, find a few reliable sources that can help you answer your questions. Write a paragraph about what you learned.

Say What?

Reading about a new region can mean learning a lot of new vocabulary. Find five words in this book you've never heard before. Use a dictionary to find out what they mean. Write the meanings in your own words. Use each word in a new sentence.

Why Do I Care?

Chapter Three discusses some of the memorials and monuments in Washington, DC. You may have never visited a national memorial or a monument. But that doesn't mean you can't think about their importance. What information can you learn from national landmarks? Why should you care about preserving them?

You Are There

This book describes the history, landmarks, and culture of the Mid-Atlantic. Imagine you are taking a trip through the region. Write a letter home telling your friends where you go and what you see along the way. Be sure to add plenty of details.

GLOSSARY

estuary
an area where a freshwater river or stream meets the ocean

gorge
a narrow valley with steep, rocky walls

industrialization
the process in which factories and manufacturing industries are developed in a region

monument
a building, pillar, or statue that honors a person or event

obelisk
a pillar with four sides that becomes narrower as it goes up and ends in the shape of a pyramid

reservation
an area of land set aside by the federal government for use by a Native American tribe

reservoir
a lake where water is collected as a water supply

stock
funds or money that are invested into a company or business

suspension bridge
a bridge in which the weight of a roadway is supported by two or more cables that pass over towers and are anchored to the ground

wetland
land that has a lot of soil moisture, such as a marsh or swamp

ONLINE RESOURCES

To learn more about the Mid-Atlantic region of the United States, visit our free resource websites below.

Visit **abdocorelibrary.com** for free Common Core resources for teachers and students, including vetted activities, multimedia, and booklinks, for deeper subject comprehension.

Visit **abdobooklinks.com** for free additional online weblinks for further learning. These links are routinely monitored and updated to provide the most current information available.

LEARN MORE

Ogintz, Eileen. *The Kid's Guide to Washington, DC*. Guilford, CT: GPP Travel, 2013.

Rissman, Rebecca. *The Declaration of Independence*. Minneapolis, MN: Abdo Publishing, 2013.

INDEX

About the Author

Samantha Bell is the author of more than 50 nonfiction books for children. She lives in the South with her family and lots of pets. She cannot wait to visit all of the other regions in the United States again.